IMAGES
of America

GILLETTE

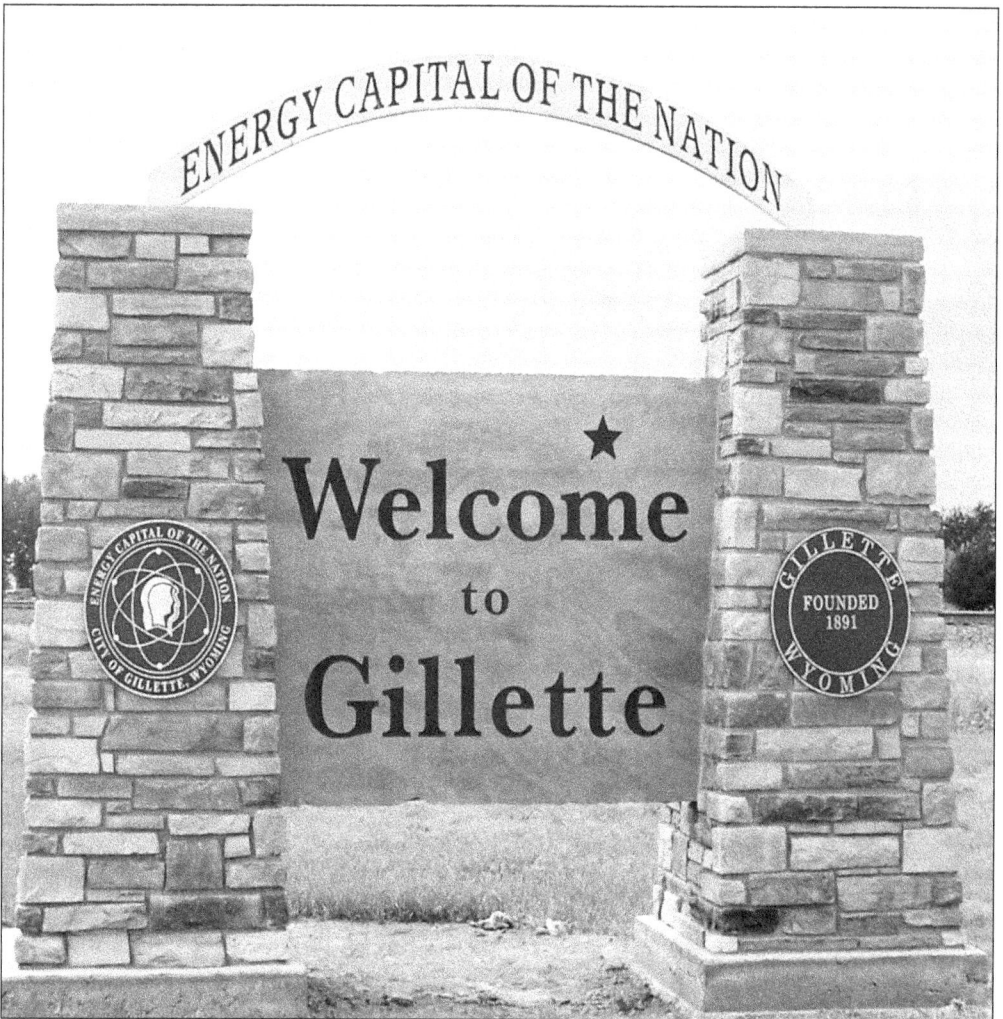

In 2009, Gillette, Wyoming, was rebounding from a relatively mild recession, when compared to the rest of the country. Wyoming state treasurer Joe Meyers said Campbell County was in an economic "garden spot," one of the few places generating income. The county's energy resources have kept local employment and spending habits somewhat stable. The minerals that make up the area's history also sustain its future. (Courtesy of the City of Gillette.)

ON THE COVER: Every summer, ranchers had a round up, separating each individual's cattle from that of other ranchers and checking for disease. In the days before fences, ranchers had to agree on ownership of unbranded calves. Many ranchers worked round ups together, as shown here in July 1901 on the Ricketts' ranch. At this camp on Horse Creek, approximately 35 miles north of Gillette, were, from left to right, Ira Wilson, W. J. Monnett, Lora Reed, Mayme Doze, Lee Wear, Mr. Ely, Ray Gilstrap (from Sheridan), John Daly, Thomas B. Ricketts, W. P. "Peter" Ricketts, and J. C. Gupton. (Courtesy of the Rockpile Museum.)

IMAGES
of America

GILLETTE

Mary Kelley with photographs from the
Campbell County Rockpile Museum

ARCADIA
PUBLISHING

Published by Arcadia Publishing
Charleston, South Carolina

Library of Congress Control Number: 2009937667

For all general information contact Arcadia Publishing at:
Telephone 843-853-2070
Fax 843-853-0044
E-mail sales@arcadiapublishing.com
For customer service and orders:
Toll-Free 1-888-313-2665

Visit us on the Internet at www.arcadiapublishing.com

This book is dedicated to my sister, Nancy,
who has yet to appreciate the beauty of
the Great Plains—but I'll keep trying!

CONTENTS

ACKNOWLEDGMENTS

My closest partners in this project were the staff of the Campbell County Rockpile Museum. Registrar Robert Henning thought of me when Arcadia Publishing called to see if he could recommend someone to write this book on Gillette. Since that time, Henning has been instrumental in proofreading the drafts, helping me choose the best photographs for this project, searching out alternatives, and e-mailing me samples so I could revise and revise and revise my layout. Museum director Terry Girouard was my liaison with his board of directors, ensuring their approval and support. I could not have undertaken a book about the history of Gillette without Henning and Girouard's help.

The rest of the museum staff welcomed me on my daily lunch-hour visits and Saturday campouts at the museum computer. The Campbell County Library staff was also involved in this project, even to the point that the reference librarians would keep an article or photograph on their desk, saving it until the next time I came in. Library director Patty Myers has always been supportive of my passion for history. I cannot thank her enough for proofing my work and offering constructive comments. The Wright Centennial Museum also lent me some pictures.

Old friends and new friends who offered photographs and stories include Rhyllis Rae Oedekoven, Marilyn Dunbar, Vicki Odegard, Bill Eisele, Randy Thomas, Lee Worman, Harriett Underwood, and Don Spielman.

Coal mine personnel also shared early photographs, including Beckie Gustafson at Belle Ayr Mine; Diane Soloman at Cordero Mine; and Jim Sutherland, Carol Jandreau, and Ken Kehn, who helped interpret those mine photographs and put a story to the picture.

I would like to thank the American Heritage Center, the National Archives, and Dana Prater at the Sheridan County Museum for making a career of having great photographs available for people like me to borrow for our unique projects.

If I have forgotten to mention anyone, I sincerely apologize and appreciate your help.

Last, but not least, I want to say thank you to my husband, Mike, and my son, Sean, who had to entertain themselves on the golf course or baseball diamond on weekends while I locked myself in our basement to work on my book. Their patience, love, and support mean everything.

All photographs are courtesy of the Campbell County Rockpile Museum, unless otherwise noted.

INTRODUCTION

Gillette's beginning was that of a typical Western cow town—rough and basic with infrastructure just substantial enough to get by. Its economy was based primarily on ranching. The dry plains were not fertile enough to support much in the way of agriculture, just enough foliage for grazing, which often required supplemental feed. The Sioux and Crow still called the Great Plains home, and the U.S. government had agreed to that in several treaties. However, the demand for additional homesteading land forced the government to relocate the Native Americans to open northeastern Wyoming, replacing them with land-hungry pioneers.

The Black Hills of Dakota were sacred to the Sioux Indians. In the Sioux Treaty of 1868, the United States recognized the Black Hills as part of the Great Sioux Reservation, set aside for exclusive use by the Sioux people. By 1874, however, Brig. Gen. George A. Custer led an expedition into the Black Hills, accompanied by miners who were looking for gold. Once gold was found in the Black Hills, miners were moving into the Sioux hunting grounds and demanding protection from the U.S. Army. The Sioux defended their land, including at the battle at Little Bighorn, where Custer was defeated. Most of Wyoming was originally part of the Dakota Territory, with the Black Hills stopping east of what would be Gillette.

Before the railroad crossed the prairie, there were few settlements or ranches in northeastern Wyoming. Open range allowed grazing of cattle, horses, and later sheep. The various homestead acts in later years provided acreage for small ranches but not enough to support the herds of cattle desired by cattle barons. Ranchers had family members claim homesteads adjoining theirs until the property was large enough to sustain livestock. When times were tough and droughts plagued the area, the smaller ranchers sold out, and the larger ranches grew. Because water was scarce, whoever controlled the water controlled the range. This history of Gillette is really a history of Campbell County because the ranchers, along with the railroad, were the reason Gillette sprang to life and has succeeded during the past 120 years.

The railroad arrived in Gillette in the summer of 1891. The first land bought on the site of Gillette was purchased by Frank Murray, Robert and George Durley, and Charles T. Weir, young men of pioneer stock and employees of the Burlington and Missouri Railroad. Their lots cost $1.25 per acre. Gillette was incorporated on January 6, 1892, and the first election was held on February 1, 1892. Herbert A. Alden was elected mayor; Levi Miller, city clerk; John T. Daly, city treasurer; and Lute and Ed Fitch were appointed marshals. The little town bustled for several years. After the railroad was built past Gillette, the railroad moved its commissary, and Gillette declined. A fire in November 1895 destroyed much of the town, leaving two saloons, two stores, and a restaurant. Pioneers continued to settle on the Great Plains, longing for a place of their own. There were few trees, fewer watering holes, and more sagebrush than grass. It was several days' ride to get supplies. Winters were frigid and windy; summers were hot and windy. Not everyone who tried a life in the West succeeded. There was, however, an abundant source of fuel—namely coal—close enough to the surface that it was easily accessible by the average person. That same coal was a hazard when spontaneous combustion occurred, and underground fires made it dangerous to walk or ride over the weakened terrain. Those same underground fires provided fuel for roasting hot dogs and brewing coffee by resourceful picnickers! Little did they know back then how important the coal would be in the growth and economic development of Gillette.

Small coal mines were built around the area as early as 1909. Most were named after the landowner, such as the Shields Mine, named for Mark Shields. The Peerless Mine was the first commercial mine in this area. The Wyodak Mine was developed in 1924, operating near the Peerless Mine in the same coal seam. Wyodak was the first surface coal mine in the world and the largest for many years. It continues to produce coal today. Other coal mines were opened in the mid-1970s, creating an unprecedented influx of workers into Gillette. Oil explorations had also been going on since the 1940s, and the first commercial discovery was made in 1948. Major discoveries in eastern Campbell County in 1956 set off an oil boom, resulting in more growth for Gillette.

This account of Gillette's history touches on many hardworking pioneer families and a smattering of rowdy characters. Cowboys used to shoot the doorknobs off stores downtown or shoot the signal lanterns of railroad workers. Colorful figures like Woodbox Jim, Rattlesnake Jack, and Fat the Barber provide stories that enliven the area's history. Many of Gillette's streets are named after pioneers such as Butler-Spaeth, Warlow, or Rohan. Even cattle brands and ranches have streets named after them, such as 4-J, Hogeye, and T-7. Included in this short history is the impact of the booms of the early 1900s, the 1950s, and the mid-1970s, as well as the effects of the busts of the 1920s and 1940s. Some declines were due to economic impacts around the country, such as the Great Depression, or were weather-related, such as the blizzard of 1949.

Many of those families who settled near Gillette and stayed through the hard times are reaping the benefits of their fortitude. While it was not a glamorous life, nor an easy life, pioneers enjoyed dances, church functions, and seeing Gillette grow from a cow town to a beautiful city. The discovery of coal, oil, or gas on area ranches has enabled pioneer families to quit their city jobs and enjoy the ranching life their ancestors envisioned.

One

DESOLATION

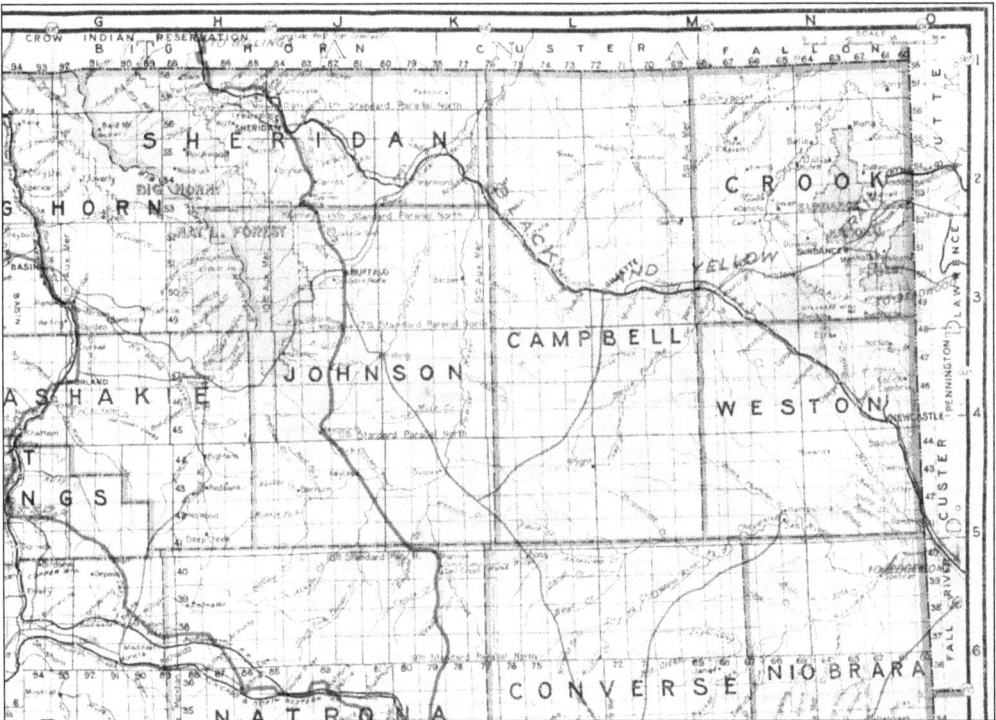

The Powder River country encompasses an area of the Great Plains between the Bighorn Mountains and the Black Hills. During the late 1860s, the area was the scene of Red Cloud's war between the Lakota and the United States. Following the end of the Great Sioux War of 1876–1877, the area was opened to white settlement, one of the last areas available for homesteading in the continental United States.

Recorded expeditions into northern Wyoming began as long ago as 1743 with the De la Venedrye brothers looking for a passage from Canada to the shores of the Western Seas. The real migration began after Col. George Armstrong Custer (shown here) explored the neighboring Black Hills for gold in 1874. The military put out the word "no gold from the grass roots down." Moses Milner, an old scout said, "There was gold from the grass roots up" meaning good grass for cattle. It was taken wrong, and the national press said there was gold from the grass roots down! The army pulled out of the area, and the gold rush was on. (Courtesy of the American Heritage Center, University of Wyoming.)

The Homestead Act of 1862 granted any U.S. citizen 160 acres of government land. For the next five years, the homesteader had to live on the land, build a 12-by-14 dwelling and grow crops. Some took advantage of a loophole, caused when those drafting the language failed to specify whether the dwelling was to be built in feet or inches. A family poses above with their wagon during their pursuit of a homestead.

The intent of the Homestead Act of 1862 was to grant land for farming. While 160 acres may have been sufficient for an Eastern farmer, it was simply not enough on the dry plains. Some ranchers filed for a homestead surrounding a water source, and then the use of that water source would be denied to other cattle ranchers, effectively closing off the adjacent public land to competition. In this photograph, more than 50 men, women, and children prepare for a round up on the 4-J Ranch around 1900.

Several treaties, such as the Treaties of Laramie 1851 and 1868, recognized the Black Hills of South Dakota and Wyoming as belonging to the Sioux and, therefore, off-limits to settlers. In those treaties, the U.S. government promised control of the Great Plains, which was the bulk of Native American territory, for "as long as the river flows and the eagle flies." The possibility of gold, however, lured the white man to the area.

Famous explorer Jim Bridger led the first wagon train into the Powder River region in 1855 and came through again with the Lt. Henry E. Maynadier/Capt. William F. Raynolds exploration in 1859–1860. Raynolds told how the name "Powder River" was arrived at from the "sulphureous vapors rising from beds of burning lignite in the vicinity whose ash was scattered up and down the river." As shown here, it could also be a challenge to drive through.

Nearly all the area of Wyoming was carved from the Territory of Dakota. Congressman William Lawrence introduced bill H.R. 86 to provide for a "temporary government for the Territory of Lincoln (Wyoming)" on March 25, 1867. The idea of a separate territory did not pass the house until July 22, 1868. An early exploration included comments from a scientist making daily notes about the area. He wrote, "The whole of this region is barren and desolate, totally unfit for the uses of civilized human beings—interesting to a geologist, and a splendid Indian country." Off in the distance, a solitary pronghorn antelope feels right at home. Wyoming has long been a state with more antelope than people.

Jacob Louie Kaufman, known affectionately as "Jew Jake," filed on a homestead on the banks of the Belle Fourche River in 1879. He established one of the first post offices in the area, known as LaBelle. His handling of the mail was not very professional. When the mail was dropped off, he emptied it onto a table and let the patrons shuffle through the pile to find theirs. One day a stranger walked in while Jake was in a poker game. The man asked for some stamps. Jake instructed him to just walk behind the bar and get the stamps out of the cigar box and put the price of the stamps in the cigar box. The stranger was a postal inspector. Jake was relieved of his postal duties. After Jake moved to Gillette, he was appointed by the Crook County commissioners to oversee the first election and the incorporation of Gillette.

On the Great Plains, where natural shelter and visible landmarks were difficult to find, the Rockpile served as a significant landmark in Campbell County. The stock trail ran near the Rockpile, so cowboys knew they were almost to the end of the trail when they saw it. In 1891, Robert and George Durley, Frank Murray, and Charles T. Weir, employees of the Lincoln Land Company, filed the first Gillette homestead applications on land that surrounded the Rockpile.

The real glamour of the West was captured in this photograph showing a pioneer woman trying to eke a living out of the prairie. As hardworking and committed to success as she was, there was a limit to what would grow and survive in the rugged climate. The best sources of water were taken by the first homesteaders. For the next round of pioneers, water was scarce on the prairie until they dug wells on their land.

Some original homes were made of logs filled in with mud and grass. The roof was made of strips of sod or prairie grass, which was plentiful on the Great Plains, where timber was scarce.

During the years of the open range, the Powder River country was described in the following cry: "The Powder River, a mile wide, an inch deep, too thick to drink, too thin to plow, an' where she flows, nobody knows!"

Two

WE WILL NAME A TOWN AFTER YOU

The original settlement in the area that would become Gillette was a small tent town on Donkey Creek, west of present-day Gillette. This community, known as Donkey Town, was a temporary base camp for survey crews from the Burlington and Missouri Railroad, who were planning to build a line through northeastern Wyoming in the late 1880s. Engineer and surveyor Edward Gillette (right) was in charge of surveying the area. (Courtesy of the Sheridan County Museum and the Coffeen family.)

The original roadbed turned south of the Wyodak coal mine and followed Donkey Creek west toward Wild Horse Creek. When there was sufficient rainfall, Wild Horse Creek spilled into the famous Powder River. Edward Gillette found a shorter route that saved the railroad 5 miles of track and 30 bridges.

When the railroad asked Gillette what he would like as compensation, he asked for a raise in pay. They turned down his request for more money but said they would name the town after him instead. Thank goodness for Edward Gillette, or this book would be entitled "Donkey Town."

Edward Gillette was a well-educated man who was born in 1854 in New Haven, Connecticut. He graduated from Sheffield Scientific School of Yale University. His work covered hundreds of miles of surveys in Nebraska, Wyoming, South Dakota, Montana, Arizona, New Mexico, and Colorado. He is shown here with his granddaughter Virginia, who called him "Grandpa Teddy."

Gillette's wife, Hallie, was the daughter of Wyoming pioneers, the Henry A. Coffeens of Sheridan. The Coffeen and Gillette families are pictured here in Sheridan. The Gillettes had two children, Harriet Selby and Edward Hollister Gillette. Edward Gillette held several state offices and maintained a private engineering practice in Sheridan, where he died on January 3, 1936. (Courtesy of the Sheridan County Museum.)

Nine months before the railroad was to arrive in Gillette, the railroad had advertised it would be ready to receive stock shipments on August 12, 1891. Early grading (shown here) was done by horse-drawn equipment. The railroad made good on its word, and the first train was loaded August 12. On August 15, 1891, the first mixed train came in, bringing passengers, mail, express, and freight. (Courtesy of the Wyoming State Archives, Department of State Parks and Cultural Resources.)

When the rails were first laid into Gillette, the railroad was the Burlington and Missouri, later called the Chicago, Burlington, and Quincy (CB&Q). To induce settlers to come to Wyoming, in 1892, the Burlington Railroad offered to carry passengers from Kansas City, Missouri, to Gillette for $2.

Dr. Norval Hamilton Baker is the first known doctor to have practiced in Gillette. He was practicing in Sundance when the railroad was building into this area. For awhile, he would see his patients in both Sundance (62 miles away) and at a field hospital 25 miles west of Gillette. In 1900, he moved his family to Gillette and practiced there until 1910, when he moved to Sheridan. He died in Sheridan in 1916.

The Burlington Beanery was a railroad "eating house" located at First Street and Gillette Avenue in the early railroad days. The well-dressed staff of the Burlington Beanery is shown here. The restaurant closed on May 1, 1922, when railroaders were being laid off as the economy declined.

This was Gillette's roundhouse—a building used by railroads for the maintenance and repair of railroad equipment. Many times the building itself was round, but sometimes the name referred to the turntable inside, which facilitated access to the train. Early steam locomotives and some passenger cars and observation cars were designed for operation in a particular direction. The turntable allowed a locomotive to be turned around for the return journey.

The roundhouse crew poses here around 1910. C. C. Chabo is believed to be the man on the far right.

With trains come accidents. This derailment of passenger train No. 42 took place on January 22, 1918. Passengers mill around looking lost as a Bucyrus crane works to right the fallen train.

Main Street in Gillette in 1891 showed a handful of frame buildings and dirt roads. With the arrival of the railroad, the town boomed almost overnight, boasting seven saloons, three dance halls, and "a matching contingent of hard-working, fast-living railway construction workers," according to the April 1, 1977, pamphlet "In Wyoming."

W. P. "Peter" Ricketts worked as the foreman for the Western Union Beef Company and later became a prominent rancher when he purchased the Half Circle L. Joining other ranchers like the Keeline family, J. A. Osborne, J. D. Collins, and Tom Matthews, Ricketts helped Gillette become one of the largest cattle shipping points in the West.

With Gillette becoming an important shipping point for the large cattle ranchers, good horses were as important as fat cattle. During the blizzard of 1891, two cowboys gave their horses their heads (let the horses lead the way), and the horses took them to a nearby camp, where they waited out the storm. This photograph shows a horse sale taking place at the Gillette stockyards in 1899.

Native American visitors and early Gillette citizens pose in front of the Daly Store on Gillette Avenue in 1895. John Thomas Daly and his brother, James H. Daly, established the first general store in the tent city of Gillette on August 12, 1891. In 1895, the store was destroyed by fire, but it was rebuilt and continued operation until 1939.

Even 20 years after the railroad came to Gillette, the four-horse team was indispensable in hauling freight. Businesses on Gillette Avenue around 1910 included Gillette Commercial, McClelland's Market, and Sutherland Plumbing.

Dr. Paul Newcomer (holding an unidentified girl) poses with Native Americans going through town around the beginning of the 20th century. Dr. Newcomer came to Gillette as a saloon keeper and gambler but left to attend medical school. He returned to practice medicine around 1905 and stayed until 1915, when he moved to California.

The interior of the Buffalo Hump Saloon was decorated with mounted trophy heads. Pictured here are, from left to right, Gillette pioneers LeRoy Montgomery, Robert Tantum, two unidentified, Otha "Ote" Spielman, two unidentified, John T. Daly, and two unidentified.

The east side of Gillette Avenue in 1902 shows, from left to right, the Derby Saloon, the Derby Billiard Parlor, the Turf Exchange Saloon, and the Dodd House (hotel). The population in 1900, just eight years after Gillette was incorporated, was 151.

William Dennis Rooney and Effie Browne Gupton celebrated their marriage in 1901 at the Gupton home, located at Third Street and Carey Avenue. Attending the celebration are, from left to right, James D. Collins, John A. Allison, William D. Rooney, Effie Gupton Rooney, Mabel Rose Morgan, and Bessie Belle Gupton.

The Hobo Band played at many social events in Gillette, especially at baseball games between the "Fats" and the "Leans." The local businessmen on the "Fats" team all weighed in at more than 200 pounds; the "Leans" team members all weighed under 200 pounds. One member of the band, Solomon Dodge "S. D." Perry (third from right), was the editor of the newspaper, the *Gillette News*, from 1904 to 1912.

Lew and Carrie Jenne lived in this neat home at the southwest corner of First Street and Kendrick Avenue around 1905.

Catherine and Grace Morgan stand on the veranda of the James T. Morgan home around 1907, when this 10-room house was built. James T. Morgan owned the general stores in Gillette and later bought and operated the Rex Theatre. He also manufactured cement blocks that were used to construct some of the early Gillette buildings, like the 1909 addition to the south side of the Goings Hotel.

The Daly mansion, shown here around 1924, would later become the Campbell County Courthouse. John T. Daly has the distinction of being the first merchant in Gillette as well as having one of the first frame buildings. He opened a general store on Gillette Avenue two days before the railroad came to town in 1891.

Lew and Ruth Barlow (pictured here in 1940) built a house on Warren Avenue in 1902, when there were only paths instead of streets. They carried water from a town pump located close to Second Street and Gillette Avenue. When Lew Barlow suggested to the mayor (either E. L. Fitch or H. H. Sandusky; both served in 1902) that a better water system would be appreciated, he was told he should have known better than to build a house out "in the country."

Many settlers brought a favorite tree or plant from their home state when they moved to the Wild West; however, some were not suited to the dry, harsh climate of northeastern Wyoming. This Rocky Mountain poppy brightened the garden of Mark and Bernice Richmond in 1919. (Courtesy of the Richmond-Oedekoven Collection.)

Otha "Ote" Spielman carried the mail from Sundance to the post office called LaBelle, near the present-day site of Moorcroft, which was operated by Jew Jake. This photograph shows Otha and his wife, Nora, in the early 1900s. Ote's older brother, Harve, was also a mail carrier from 1897 to 1899 on the route from Gillette to Powderville, Montana, a distance of 125 miles, which took three days and three teams of horses.

Harve and Elizabeth (Musselman) Spielman are shown here around 1892, the year they were married. When he was not delivering the mail, Harve and his crew built some of the nicer homes in early Gillette, including those of Harry Chassell and J. T. Morgan, and the John Daly house.

Gillette, Wyo.
1912

These two scenes show Gillette Avenue looking north, with the above photograph showing the west side of the street and the image below showing the east side. In a flyer advertising life in Gillette just a few years prior, it was noted that the "streets and side-walks are above reproach and the drainage system is almost perfect. The residence portion of the city is replete with beautiful and costly houses, denoting enterprise and thrift on the part of the people."

Gillette, Wyo.
1912

Three

NOT JUST A COW TOWN

When Harry Chassell came to this territory, Weston and Campbell Counties had not yet been created out of Crook County. Chassell was one of the first permanent settlers in Gillette, coming here in 1891 from Sundance, where he had taught school for almost four years. This photograph shows Chassell in 1911, when he was a member of the state legislature representing Crook County. He introduced the bill that created Campbell County out of Crook and Weston Counties, which was approved by the state legislature on February 13, 1911. (Courtesy of the Wyoming State Archives, Department of State Parks and Cultural Resources.)

Wyoming had 14 counties when Campbell County was formed by the 11th Wyoming Legislature, along with Goshen, Hot Springs, Lincoln, Niobrara, Platte, and Washakie Counties. It was named for two Campbells: Robert Campbell, who was with William Henry Ashley's expedition in this part of the country from 1825 to 1835; and also John A. Campbell, the first territorial governor. Harry Chassell (shown here in 1935) had an active political career until he retired to Wisconsin in 1958. (Courtesy of the Wyoming State Archives, Department of State Parks and Cultural Resources.)

Lew G. Butler was the first sheriff of Campbell County, from 1913 to 1914. He hailed from Omaha, where he worked as a broncobuster and cowboy. He knew the West better than most, having trailed cattle from the Gulf of Mexico to Canada. Butler retired to California after having spent 40 years bucking the winters of Wyoming.

The Rockpile has long been a place to meet, court, play, and picnic. Names and dates carved in the stone are still visible, although the Rockpile is now behind a protective fence. Bernice Orton (seated) and an unidentified woman pose in a crevice of the Rockpile in 1919. (Courtesy of the Richmond-Oedekoven Collection.)

The Gillette Post Office moved from business to business, depending on who the postmaster was at the time. In this photograph, dated December 8, 1912, the postmaster was Lola Smith (second from left). This building is still at 221 South Gillette Avenue.

Following several years of ranching, Alexander Bright Maycock and his brother, Joseph Michael Maycock, started Stockmen's Bank on January 7, 1907. The Maycock brothers, together with William R. Wright, John A. Allison, and N. W. Chassell, put their own money together to total the $10,000 minimum capital required by state law to become a new bank. The bank was in business until 1987.

Alex Maycock (left) and M. R. Hunter (right) are in a relaxed pose inside Stockmen's Bank around 1907. Maycock was elected in 1941 to a two-year term as Campbell County's representative in the state legislature, and in 1943, he was chosen to be the county representative of the state senate until 1947. Joe Maycock built the house on the corner of Ross Avenue and Fourth Street in 1910, but he preferred life on the ranch located 25 miles west of Gillette.

Two Sunday schools join together—one from the Cook home and one from the Barkley home—to make the beginning of the Bethlehem Community Church south of Gillette. Dora Haden was active in the Bethlehem Community Church and, as a teacher, was asked to organize a new school around 1918. She named it the New Hope School, which held Sunday school services for the Bethlehem church until a church building could be constructed in 1922.

The early history of the Catholic Church in Gillette is tied closely to that of the railroad. The first priest, Rev. P. G. Cassidy, visited Gillette in 1892 after the railroad came through in August 1891. The congregation of 12 members met for Mass at the Burlington section house. There was an early Catholic church built in 1906. St. Matthews Catholic Church, pictured here, was built in 1951 on Gillette Avenue.

Holy Trinity Episcopal Church is the oldest church still in existence in Gillette. It is located at 610 South Kendrick Avenue and is currently painted white.

The Reverend Samuel C. Ryland was the much-loved pastor at First Presbyterian Church from 1920 until 1947, when he resigned due to poor health. The church was organized in 1913 and was served by several pastors until Reverend Ryland came. The congregation attended this church, located at Fourth Street and Kendrick Avenue, until the present-day church was built in 1962 at Fifth Street and Carey Avenue.

William Underwood worked as a carpenter, blacksmith, barber, and in the livery barn. When he ordered lumber to finish building a school in 1892, he found himself in the lumber business. Underwood Lumber built the first addition on the Goings Hotel, the Bank of Gillette, and several other structures in early Gillette.

The William Underwood family portrait includes, from left to right, (first row) Ethel Underwood, Martha Underwood, Irma Underwood (seated in front), William Underwood, and William H. Underwood; (second row) Lloyd Underwood, Newell Underwood, Hazel Underwood, and Roy Underwood. The photograph was taken around 1913.

The Bank of Gillette started in 1902, making it Gillette's first organized bank. It occupied a small frame building downtown until 1920, when "Gillette's million-dollar bank" was constructed. The Edelman Drug Store occupied this building as of June 1935. The Edelman family still owns this impressive building today, which now houses Pat's Hallmark, at the corner of Second Street and Gillette Avenue. (Courtesy of Randy Thomas.)

The first Gillette Women's Club (pictured above) was formed before 1920 and boasted members from the most prominent families in Gillette. The Cates, Chabo, Chassell, Fitch, Gupton, Culavin, Underwood, Barlow, Morgan, and Daly women were among the early members. A cemetery association was formed by the women's club in June 1922 for the purpose of "caring for our local burying ground." A meeting was held of "all who have loved ones buried here." Yearly dues for the cemetery association members was set at $1, to be used to keep the cemetery in good condition. The oldest marked grave at Mount Pisgah, Gillette's only cemetery, is for Sallie Newell, who died on June 4, 1904. There are older graves, but they are marked only with the name of the deceased and no date. This photograph of the cemetery was taken in 1908 by Julia E. Tuell when there were four marked graves. (Below, courtesy of the Campbell County Cemetery Board.)

William Robert Wright, the mayor of Gillette from 1928 to 1930, spent several years of his youth in an orphanage. He rose from humble beginnings to own 64,000 acres, raising cattle and sheep, and was interested in soil conservation. He was named provincial commissioner by the governor to organize Campbell County. He was a representative in the Wyoming legislature, chairman of the Selective Service Board during World War II, and a member of the Campbell County High School Board. He was president of Stockmen's Bank and belonged to the Knights Templar Lodge, the Lions Club, and the Baptist Church.

This was the Wright Post Office in 1906, with Richard Wright as postmaster. The post office moved from place to place until it was closed in 1942. However, the "new" town of Wright reactivated the charter in August 1976 as the town grew around the Wright and Reno properties.

The Keeline family started with George Frederick Keeline, a native of Germany who came to Wyoming in 1874. His sons, grandsons, and nephews continued ranching operations in Campbell and Weston Counties using brands such as "Hogeye," "Flying Circle," and "TY"—one of the oldest brands in the state.

1911.
Gillette, Wyo.

The Keelines ran both cattle and sheep. Shown here is the Keeline Sheep Company, in operation around 1900, when the family owned 33,000 sheep. The hard winter of 1911 meant the loss of 22,000 sheep on just the Keeline ranches.

When the T7 cattle brand followed the Texas Trail and crossed the Wyoming border in 1881, the T7 operation came into existence and has remained in Wyoming since. It is thought the "T7" name originated from "T" for Thomas Newton or "T. N." Matthews, and the "7" for the seven members of his immediate family. Round ups, like this one in 1901, were held every summer. After one particularly hard winter, the few remaining T7 cattle were found in the breaks around the Belle Fourche River, and this led to the selection of that location for the ranch and its headquarters.

One of the pioneer families in Campbell County was the Edward and Phoebe (Matthews) Fitch family. Edward Fitch must have had an exceptional ranch, as an article in *History of Wyoming*, volume III, published in 1918, said, "He has since given his attention to the livestock business and is today the owner of a large and splendidly improved ranch property, the neat and thrifty appearance of which indicates his careful supervision, his progressive methods and his spirit of undaunted enterprise." Edward Fitch was Gillette's mayor from 1901 to 1902.

C. Glenn Fitch, born on December 28, 1892, the son of Edward and Phoebe Fitch, was the first white child born in Gillette. One of Glenn's sons, William (shown here), lived all his life in Gillette with his wife, Helen. Together, they have been instrumental in developing Gillette's children's developmental center, public health nursing program, recreation center, and senior center. William died on October 9, 2009.

In 1918, William O. "Bill" and Willa Mae Bishop ran several thousand sheep, 200 head of horses, and 37 Hereford cows. Many ranchers tried raising more than one type of livestock. Sheep were popular with some because of the two possible income sources—wool and meat. By 1943, the Bishop ranch was an all-cattle operation.

The livery barn of yesteryear was the counterpart of the service station of today. There were a few makeshift liveries in the early days, but in 1898, George Fox built a barn specifically for that purpose. Fox and his son-in-law Lora Reed operated it for some time, followed by William D. Rooney and Andrew S. French. Clarence "Spike" Haigler also operated it for several years. This photograph was taken when it was known as Haigler's Livery. The livery burned in November 1921, damaging the Goings Hotel next door.

Hamilton "Hamp" Smith built a livery barn at Second Street and Kendrick Avenue. He later sold it to Simon P. Hardy. In 1926, the Saunders family bought it and turned it into a lumberyard. This photograph shows Simon "Dad" Hardy standing beside his daughter Winnie (on horseback). The fellow in the wagon is unidentified.

Standing in front of Saunders Lumber Company are, from left to right, Don Saunders, Walter Boone Saunders, unidentified, Bob Saunders, and Dell Lane. The company was started on November 1, 1921, when the W. B. Saunders family moved here from Billings, Montana, to assume ownership of the Logan Lumber Company. In those early days, at Christmas, the company gave every widow in Gillette a pick-up load of kindling, split and ready for use.

Frank Olzer's Saddle Shop was built in 1908 and was the forerunner to other saddle and boot shops. After a series of owners, Lawrence "LJ" Probst took over in the mid-1920s. L. J.'s father, Bill, was a maker of wooden shoes for a Dutch community in Illinois. L. J. followed in his father's footsteps and went into the shoe business in Gillette.

Nellie Tayloe Ross, governor of Wyoming, visited Gillette during the Campbell County Fair in 1926. All of Gillette's north-south downtown streets are named for Wyoming governors, with the exception of Gillette Avenue. The Business and Professional Women's Club petitioned the city council to change the street names in 1930 from names thought to be confusing to names of governors, including Ross Street. (Courtesy of the Wyoming State Archives, Department of State Parks and Cultural Resources.)

This scene is sheep skinning at the Guthrie ranch following the blizzard of 1911. Taking part were, from left to right, Charlie Guthrie, Josie Music, a Mrs. Barrett, and Alverta Barrett. Many ranchers incurred huge losses due to severe winter weather. Other years noted for severe winters were 1880, 1915, 1922, and 1949. The blizzard of 1949 dropped only 8 inches of snow, but temperatures were as low as 12 below zero, with high winds for 60 hours.

An unidentified man poses with a little girl in front of a snowbank after the blizzard of April 1912. Notice the snow is up to the roof of the house behind them.

Pigs rummage in the wreckage left at George Ward's place after a tornado struck in July 1928, four miles east of Gillette. Tornados are relatively rare in northeastern Wyoming.

If natural disasters were not enough, man-made events could also wreck havoc on Gillette's pioneers. This CB&Q livestock car tipped on a broken trestle. Six men worked with cables to right the car again.

A Campbell County fair was the dream of L. P. McVay, a homesteader living south of Gillette in 1916. He built a school building for his daughters to attend and interested his neighbors in holding a county fair in the schoolhouse. Gillette merchants donated prizes, the Gillette City Band performed, races were held, and a few hardy souls put on a rodeo for entertainment.

Behind this happy couple are the fairgrounds that grew from McVay's dream. The county fair outgrew its little schoolhouse, south of Gillette, in just a few years. It was then moved to the Savageton Hall and finally to Gillette, where there was a large piece of land just east of the Rockpile. People watched the fair activities and rodeos from the Rockpile for many years. Jess and Pearl Boardman had this photograph taken on their wedding day in 1935.

Four

No Commercial Value

In his *Annual Report of the Territorial Geologist to the Governor of Wyoming 1890*, Louis D. Ricketts (pictured) wrote, "The coal of this district has little other use than that of supplying a local market," referring to parts of the Powder River field. Other parts of the Powder River field had been identified as having huge coal reserves. It would be more than 30 years before a mine was developed for commercial coal sales. (Courtesy of the American Heritage Center, University of Wyoming.)

Louis Ricketts, a territorial geologist, wrote, "The numerous settlers have almost always a cheap and convenient fuel at hand. . . . This fire is quite well known to the inhabitants of this location, the heat from these fissures being used for the roasting of wieners and the heating of coffee." Above, local residents enjoy the warmth of a nearby coal fire. (Courtesy of the Richmond-Oedekoven Collection.)

Four four-horse teams pull fresno scrapers (earth movers) at the Peerless Coal Company in 1924. Work at the mine began in 1922 by a company of men who believed Campbell County coal could be sold on the market in competition with other coal mined in Wyoming and Montana. How right they were!

This opening in the ground is most likely an entrance to an underground coal mine, possibly the Peerless Mine. The Peerless underground mine was west of the present-day PacifiCorp power plant. The Peerleess Mine included a tipple, 13 dwellings, a store, a boardinghouse, and an office building. The mine employed 30 men. The mine had a rocky start, opening and closing several times from 1922 to 1924. Mine inspector records show the mine was idle in 1925, 1926, and 1927. (Courtesy of the Wyodak Resources Development Corporation.)

The Homestake Mining Company bought the Peerless Mine and converted it from an underground mine to a surface mine. It became part of the Wyodak property. For many years, it was the largest surface coal mine in the world. In this photograph, an unidentified man is operating a water cannon system, called hydrosluicing, at the Wyodak Mine on June 25, 1928. This water cannon method was used to dissolve soil around harder minerals, but it is not known how the cannon is being used in this image. Notice the mine pit to the right. (Courtesy of the Wyodak Resources Development Corporation.)

This photograph shows a steam shovel loading the conveyor hopper in the Wyodak pit, most likely around August 1928. During the Depression years, the saying was, "The last man on the job was fired." Since jobs were scarce, everyone was on time! (Courtesy of the Wyodak Resources Development Corporation.)

The Wyodak pit is shown here on November 22, 1927. The conveyor system to remove coal has been in use at this company almost from the beginning and continues today. (Courtesy of the Wyodak Resources Development Corporation.)

After the overburden or dirt is removed from the coal, a drill rig makes a series of holes into the coal. Men pack explosives into the holes, which are then connected to a cord, and the charge is lit. (Courtesy of the Wyodak Resources Development Corporation.)

This photograph shows a five-hole blast at the Wyodak Mine. The charge loosens the coal so it can be mined. A similar process is used today. (Courtesy of the Wyodak Resources Development Corporation.)

The Wyodak Coal Company was once considered to have the largest coal vein in the United States. It is still acknowledged as the longest continually operating surface mine in the country. (Courtesy of the Wyodak Resources Development Corporation.)

CB&Q or Burlington Route railroad cars are loaded with coal at the Wyodak Coal and Manufacturing Company on September 28, 1928. The number of cars a locomotive could pull in the early days was less than today. In 2009, trains often exceeded 100 cars. (Courtesy of the Wyodak Resources Development Corporation.)

The town of Wyodak existed so employees could live close to the Wyodak Coal Company. The town began around 1925. When the company planned to mine where the town was located, the houses were gradually moved, one by one, to other locations in the 1960s. (Courtesy of the Wyodak Resources Development Corporation.)

Teacher Muriel Holtz and 10 students pose at the Wyodak elementary school. The town also included a range of other businesses to serve its residents. Hardly a cement block in the original site of the town of Wyodak exists today.

This photograph shows the Bank of Gillette around 1910. Mark Shields (right) was president of the bank, mayor of Gillette, and vice president and treasurer of the Peerless Coal Mine. During the period of his presidency, the bank became recognized as one of the strongest institutions in the state of Wyoming. As a result of some bad business decisions concerning the Peerless Mine, Shields took his life in March 1923. Discrepancies were found in the bank books, resulting in the closure of the bank.

The Farmer's Cooperative Association was formed in 1923 but was not incorporated until 1928. The first grain elevator was erected in 1928 when Ben Powell leased some land east of Gillette Avenue on First Street from the railroad and financed its construction. Before the co-op, the Campbell County Farmers Marketing Union was organized by a handful of local farmers who agreed to sell their grain as a group. (Courtesy of Lee Worman.)

In the late 1930s, when automobiles were commonplace, the co-op opened this service station at Second Street and Brooks Avenue. When more pumps were needed to keep up with Gillette's growth, the co-op sold this property and built a larger service station on Highway 59. (Courtesy of Lee Worman.)

Gillette was the site of Camp Miller, a Civilian Conservation Camp (CCC), established by Pres. Franklin D. Roosevelt on March 31, 1933. Although the other 1,450 CCC camps were engaged in work in national forests and in national and state parks, this particular camp was established on May 4, 1934, for the purpose of fighting coal fires that for years had been destroying the coal veins in northeastern Wyoming. This photograph shows camp workers operating mining equipment to put out coal fires.

Dan Prentice
Project-Supt.

W. K. King
2nd. Lt. F.A. Res.
2nd. Command

COMPAN
CIVILIAN CON̄S
CAMP
Gillete, W
July 2

Bryan All
1st. Lt. F.A
Sub. Dist. C

With the exception of 23 local Wyoming boys, all the members of the CCC camp were from Texas. Those boys from the wide-open spaces of the west immediately caught the true spirit of the emergency conservation work and showed a remarkable willingness to meet any emergency,

CORPS

Walter D. Johnson
1st. Lt., Cav-Res.,

day or night. Consequently, friendly relations existed among the workmen, the camp officers, the ranchers, and the residents of the community. When World War II started in 1941, the CCC camp was abandoned, and most of the young men enlisted in the armed services.

A dozen or more coal fires burned in Little Thunder Basin, Wyoming, making Gillette the logical place for the location of a camp. Through the cooperation of the mayor and town council, the sewer, light, and water facilities of the town were made available to the camp, which was located from Fourth Street to Twelfth Street and 4-J Road. One of the reasons the camp was so successful was that the superintendent and 12 foremen were selected from the various coalfields of Wyoming, with years of experience in coal mining and its related problems. Here men work with pick and shovel to extinguish fires by extracting the coal and filling the cavities with dirt.

Tents make up the lodging for CCC camp workers before the barracks were built around 1934–1935.

This aerial photograph, dated July 12, 1938, shows the diamond shape of the rodeo arena at the county fairgrounds at the lower left, Camp Miller at the top right, and the Burlington Ditch running from the upper left through the city to the lower right. The Rockpile is in the lower right corner.

The Burlington Ditch was finished in 1908 to bring water 9 miles from Donkey Creek, southwest of Gillette, to Burlington Lake, northeast of Gillette, down to the railroad and the stockyards. The ditch ran through the residential section of downtown Gillette, including Warren Avenue (shown here). The ditch was filled in around 1948.

The Experimental Farm, now known as Cam-Plex Park, was created in the 1920s by the University of Wyoming to test which trees, grasses, and forage crops grew best in this area. Leland Landers was the superintendent of the farm from 1947 until 1980, when the university closed the farm. As superintendent, Landers planted 800 to 1,200 different grasses and crops each year to see what worked best. He; his wife, Gladys; and one full-time employee also raised cattle. Most of the buildings photographed above in the late 1960s or early 1970s are no longer there. Two that are still here are the long building to the right, now the Cam-Plex Park shop, and the building above the shop, which is the WPA building. It was known as "the Hall" and was used for dances. To the left of the WPA building was the Landers' house. The house to the far left was where the hired hand lived. Clyde Potter's property was on the other side of the railroad tracks and the single row of trees at the top of the photograph. (Courtesy Leland Landers.)

Five

BOOM AND BUST

The cycle of boom and bust has been symbolic of Gillette's history. It was suspected that oil would be discovered at some time, but it is difficult to tell when the first strike was. An unidentified man is shown here working a wildcat well in Rozet in the early 1920s. A wildcat well is one drilled into an area that does not have a proven oil field. In October 1935, the *News-Record* ran a story that oil would be sought close to Gillette in the near future. In December of that year, it was reported that the first part of an oil rig had been delivered. The drilling site was to be 16 miles southwest of Gillette. Those first wells were dry, which had to be disappointing, as speculation had been rampant for years that oil would be found in Campbell County.

The huge Belle Creek oil strike was made north of Gillette in 1955, and the Dead Horse field was discovered at the Johnson-Campbell county line in the 1950s. Later came the Hi-Lite discovery in 1967 and the Hartzog Draw field near Pumpkin Buttes in 1977.

City hall in the 1930s was a small building on Gillette Avenue. The city jail, built in 1911, was located behind city hall. The old city hall was used as a community building for church services, dances, and public meetings. It was also the morgue. When one of the departed was being kept there until burial, he or she would be moved to the old jail while a dance or meeting was held.

City hall opened at 400 South Gillette Avenue in October 1936. The building housed city government offices and the fire department. When the old fire siren would sound, firefighters would telephone the operator to see where the fire was located. The telephone lines would get so busy with everyone in town calling about the fire that firefighters had to give a code word to get the location. Most city departments moved out in 1978, when the city bought the old post office at Third Street and Gillette Avenue for temporary offices while waiting for the current city hall to be finished in 1984.

Firefighters pose with engine No. 1 of the Gillette Fire Department, when it was located at city hall at Fourth Street and Gillette Avenue, currently the City Hall Mall. Pictured from left to right are (kneeling) Dick Brown, Eugene Warlow, and Andy Oliver; (standing) Chief Charley Tyrrell, E. Z. Bay, A. G. Laughlin, Preston Gilstrap, Dale Johnson, Glen Tholson, Ray Cates, and Jim Cates Jr. This photograph was taken on May 12, 1964.

Gillette's second schoolhouse would one day become Campbell County's first courthouse. From 1913 to 1914, the courthouse was at Kendrick Avenue and Fourth Street in this one-story frame school building, constructed in 1902.

The Daly mansion was built in 1911 and was sold to the county for $16,500 in the late 1920s. It opened as the courthouse on May 4, 1928. The first library in town was in the attic. It was open only on Saturdays for the first two years. In 1965, the state fire marshal declared the old courthouse unsafe, since the second floor had only one exit. The last jury trial, held in June 1969, was held in a horse barn on the old Campbell County fairgrounds, because the presiding judge would not hold the trial in an unsafe facility.

The news article announcing the opening of the Fiesta Theatre on February 1, 1935, proclaimed "Dazzling streaks of light, shooting toward the heavens, will herald the opening, at seven o'clock tomorrow evening, of the new Fiesta Theatre in Gillette." The transformation from the Rex Theatre to the Fiesta Theatre cost owner E. J. Schulte nearly $25,000. The first movie shown was Will Rogers's super-comedy *Judge Priest*. The theater's popularity continued into the 1960s, as shown here.

Student Steven Fay receives a notebook and other free gifts at the Fiesta Theatre's back-to-school show in the early 1960s. Handing him his notebook is Bob Larson, from KIML radio, while Roy Mapel, the station announcer, interviews Fay. Behind Mapel is theater manager Al Sorenson.

Fire destroyed the Fiesta Theatre on February 17, 1964. The Fiesta Barbershop, located in the front of the theater, was also destroyed that day. Note the marquee with the movie playing that night—*The Wheeler Dealer*, starring James Garner and Lee Remick.

The Campbell County Fire Department fought this blaze for hours, but the building was destroyed. The fire also caused extreme damage to buildings on either side.

Pictured here is the west 200 block of Gillette Avenue. The center building was the second location of Stockmen's Bank. The two bank safes are still inside, even though the bank moved from this site in 1959. Gillette Pharmacy, to the right, was operated by Dr. Tom Cassidy from 1908 to 1937, when Ray Ritter purchased the building and started Ritter's Drug. Dr. Cassidy was considered such a valued resident of the community that the city named Cassidy Airfield after him.

Mike Enzi owned NZ Shoes, a downtown Gillette business from 1969 to the late 1980s. Enzi expanded his father's shoe business from one location in Sheridan to Gillette and later to Miles City, Montana. Enzi was elected mayor of Gillette in 1974 at the age of 30 and held the position for two terms. He was elected to the Wyoming House of Representatives and served from 1987 to 1991, when he was elected to the Wyoming Senate. He was elected to the U.S. Senate in 1996. He still calls Gillette home when he is in Wyoming.

At one time, Gillette had a small J. C. Penney store on Gillette Avenue. The store window is pictured here with photographs of Gillette servicemen serving in World War II.

The inscription on this Gillette Avenue monument reads, "Campbell County War Memorial. To all those who served our country in time of war. These gave their lives." Names are listed for those who paid the ultimate sacrifice in World War I, World War II, and the Korean Conflict. The monument was erected in 1955 by the VFW Auxiliary. Pictured here are Bessie Yokom, chapter president, placing a wreath as Irene Hoel, chaplin, offers a prayer on Veterans Day in 1964.

Subdivisions and mobile home parks were developed by energy companies to accommodate the workforce needed for these businesses. In 1976, almost 40 percent of Gillette's residents lived in mobile homes. A report produced by the Campbell County Chamber of Commerce in 1975 showed 30 mobile home parks in the city limits.

With additional housing needs came quality-of-life issues. In March 1961, Mayor Denzil J. "Peanuts" Dalbey attended the groundbreaking ceremony for the new public swimming pool. The pool was opened on August 1, 1961, at a cost of $63,000. Mayor Dalbey took a dive in the new pool—fully dressed—as part of the opening ceremonies.

On the prairie that was Gillette, trees were in short supply. Hundreds were planted in the open space behind the old high school, now Twin Spruce Junior High School. The City of Gillette created City Park in that spot, which today includes a shelter, a playground, the city pool, and many shade trees.

The grain elevator on the left was built in 1928 and was owned and operated by the Farmer's Cooperative Association. The new elevator on the right was built in 1961 and had twice the 12,000-bushel capacity as the old elevator. The railroad ran just behind the elevators. Railcars were originally loaded by shovel, but later they were loaded by a tube lowered from the top of the elevator.

The new Vo-Ag building at the Campbell County High School cost $100,000. The vocational section acquired new lathes, drill presses, and saws. The agricultural section had feed bunkers and horse trailers—all built by students. The addition to the high school opened on April 28, 1960.

For many years, the Gillette Graded School was the only grade school in Gillette. There were enough students for two classes in each grade, one through eight. When space ran out, three mobile classrooms were added. Part of the building cracked, and it had to be torn down around 1981. It was located on Kendrick Avenue between Fourth and Fifth Streets.

In the early 1960s, Northside Elementary and Westside Elementary were built. Westside Elementary (shown here with bare surroundings) later became the alternative high school known as Westwood.

First Presbyterian Church, at 511 Carey Avenue, is pictured here under construction in 1962. Other churches that expanded or built during Gillette's boom years are Church of Christ and First Southern Baptist Church.

Known as the Northeastern Wyoming Nursing Home, the Northeastern Wyoming Rest and Care Home, and the Northeastern Wyoming Retirement and Care Home, this facility for long-term care was needed when it was built in 1965. Ten acres of land were donated by Campbell County for the home's site, near the hospital. The facility is now known as Pioneer Manor.

During the early days of Gillette, doctors' offices were in the Hotel Newell; in houses on Gillette, Ross, and Warren Avenues; or in a building at First Street and Kendrick Avenue. In June 1953, a 31-bed, redbrick building was constructed in Gillette at a cost of $275,000. Four physicians and one visiting surgeon served the community, with a population of 2,190, which was then on the brink of an oil boom. The hospital was located at Seventh Street and Rohan Avenue.

Growth and technology go hand-in-hand, resulting in the availability of better transportation. Tommy Matthews operated Gillette Airways in the 1940s, and Jim Fulkerson offered his Fulkerson Aviation Training Fleet (pictured here) in January 1964. Pictured from left to right are (in front) an Aztec B; (middle) a Commanche and a Cherokee; and (in back) a Super Cub and a Colt.

The stock pens at the Gillette Livestock Exchange on First Street were in use from about the time the railroad came to town until the yards closed in 1977. This photograph was taken in June 1964 from the catwalk built over the pens. Tens of thousands of cattle and horses were sold at the Gillette stockyards.

80

Six

HISTORY CLASS

The Gillette grade school classes pose for a group photograph in 1902. Perhaps two of these little girls were the first two graduates of Campbell County High School in 1912. Those graduates were Gladys Perry Miller and Margaret Gibson Potts.

Mark G. Richmond and Bernice Orton Richmond are pictured here shortly after they were married in 1921. Mark was one of the Gillette residents in the regular army in World War I. Upon his return from the service, he and Bernice both taught school in the Campbell County School District. Mark taught chemistry and physics and led the pep band, while Bernice taught music and one of the graded classes. (Courtesy of the Richmond-Oedekoven Collection.)

The Campbell County School Board is shown here in 1925. Pictured are, from left to right, (first row) W. O. Bishop, J. W. Hanson, Theodore A. Wanerus, and Charles P. Berry; (second row) N. D. Morgan, Supt. Dick Wright, William Wright, B. J. Reno, and W. P. Parks.

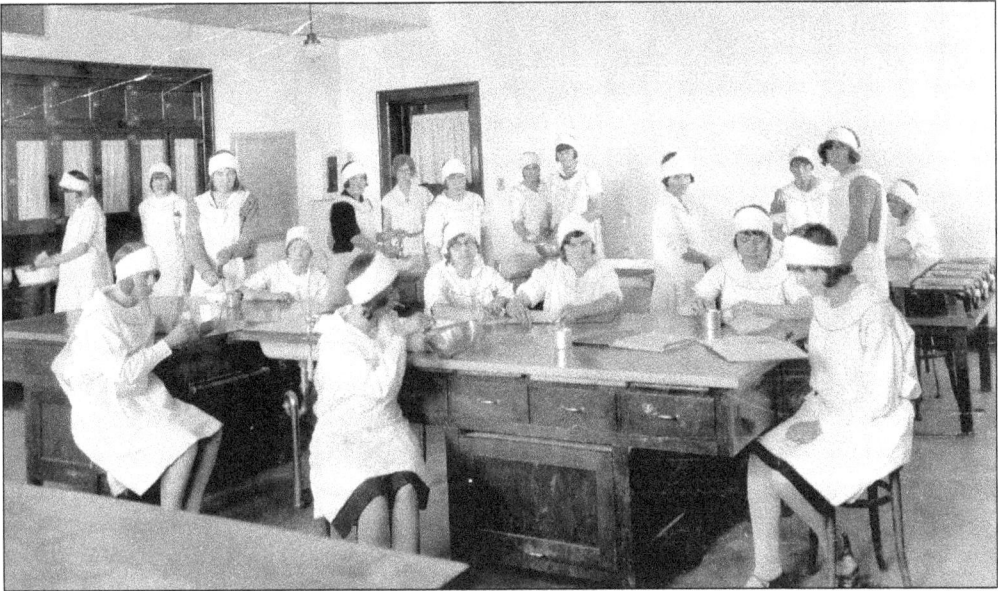

The 1930 *Camel* yearbook highlighted several vocational classes available to students, including this home economics class. There was also a Home Economics Club, organized during the 1925–1926 school year. Girls who had completed one year of home economics or who were enrolled that year were eligible to be in the club. Club activities included a bake sale, the proceeds of which went to fill a Thanksgiving basket for a needy family.

Campbell County High School students participated in more than sporting events. These eight young ladies pose in dance costumes outside the high school. From left to right are Leota Nichols, Beth Longnecker, Eileen Doud, Elynor Marshall, Rosalie Camblin, Alberta Culavin, Vera Wagner, and Emma Lou Oliver.

There were many small schools on area ranches that provided an education to local children who lived too far from Gillette to go to town everyday. Ranch owner Fred Whitten hauled 16-foot logs from Bitter Creek to build this school. The Williams, Lloyds, and Whiten children were taught at the Whitten schoolhouse around 1925. From left to right are Jane Williams, Thelma Williams, Nellie Williams, and Zella Whitten. All four girls shown here are eighth graders. Their teacher, Florence Miner, is not pictured.

Cottonwood Valley Elementary School was another small rural school, located close to Rozet. Children packed their lunches in lard pails and took quart jars of water to drink.

The first annual Northeast Wyoming Basketball Tournament was hosted by Gillette in 1925. Eight teams participated: Gillette, Rozet, Moorcroft, Upton, Sheridan, Sundance, Buffalo, and Newcastle.

Girls' sports abounded also, including this 1927 Campbell County girls' basketball team. Pictured from left to right are (first row) Doris "Dimp" Sutherland, Eva Butler, teacher Viva Kumon, unidentified, and Wilma Vasey; (second row) Vivian Sutherland, unidentified, Ava Dooley, Helen Bradbury, and Marguerite Brough.

In 1929, the Campbell County football team included, from left to right, (first row) Milo Haight, Don Harris, LeRoy Christinck, Frank Hicks, Frank Butler, Joe Maycock, Glenn Harrod, and Hank Saunders; (second row) Roy Ritter, Harold Atterbury, Dutch Sutherland, Reid Barney, Harold Campbell, Urban Bury, Archie Lindsey, Paul Norfolk, and coach D. O. Wolfenberger; (third row) Kenneth Byrum, Kenneth Bennick, John Givens, Earl Throne, and unidentified.

Gillette's Junior American Legion baseball team was organized in 1964 and is still going strong today. Pictured from left to right are (first row) Steve Hughes, Lee Gaskill, Ford Nicholson, and Benny Lara; (second row) coach Don Grace, Mickey McCormack, Tom Eskew, Ed Roberts, Nelson Miller, and Alex Henson. Vic Edwards is not pictured.

Gillette was the 1958 state basketball champs! From left to right are coach George Dorrington, Larry Bray, John Mooney, Gordon Niswender, Kenny Wolf, Harry Ilsley, Lee Fawcett, Darryl Lynde, Eddie Swartz, Darrell Coulter, Larry Taylor, Jerry Record, and John Mankin.

The 1964 Gillette West Junior High wrestling team won the first place trophy in the nine-team invitational tournament. From left to right are (kneeling) Dan Lubken, Dick Garst, Mick Shober, and Chuck Edwards; (standing) assistant coach Benny Lara, David Lynch, coach Dub Garst, Bob Marquiss, Kelly Burch, Dave Eldridge, Gene Clements, and coach Danny Kistler.

Homecoming in 1961 was a special time for Queen Betty Leonard (center) and her two attendants, Beverly Hayden (right) and D'Ann Watsabaugh (left).

Not everyone played organized sports, but they worked hard at sporting events nonetheless. The 1961 "A" cheerleading squad consisted of Donna Gaye Atwood (front), Sherryl Hoblit (left), Bonnie Carter (back), and Diane Dorrington (right).

Seven

BETWEEN THE BLACK HILLS AND YELLOWSTONE

A circus came to town sometime after 1915, bringing with it Alice, the elephant. Another act mentioned in the newspaper coverage was an aerial artist who dove into a tub of water. Gillette was on the "Black and Yellow Trail," Highway 14 that started in Chicago, Illinois, and followed an earlier road from the Black Hills of South Dakota to Yellowstone National Park. The Black and Yellow Trail brought tourists and traveling entertainers through Campbell County.

Gillette offered several options for overnight lodging. The Hotel Newell was one of those options in 1908. Ollie Ricks Crane is on horseback in front of the hotel on Second Street.

What a great postcard, reporting a "warm reception" in Gillette, meant to entice other visitors to this fair town. Old postcards from Gillette have been surprisingly popular by collectors. (Courtesy of Randy Thomas.)

In 1902, Al Dodd bought two lots on Gillette Avenue and built the Dodd House, a hotel, restaurant, and bar. It had 24 sleeping rooms. In 1905, Sam and Maggie Goings (pictured here) bought the hotel and renamed it "The Goings House." They also bought the livery next to the hotel, plus the surrounding lots, probably with expansion in mind. In 1908 or 1909, they added on to the south end of the building using cement blocks manufactured by J. T. Morgan. A fire in the livery barn destroyed the barn on Thanksgiving Day in 1921. The blaze also damaged the hotel and other nearby businesses. The original building was torn down in 1937 and rebuilt as it is today. The Goings was considered the third leg of the "Bermuda Triangle," a local legend that included the Montgomery Bar and the Center Bar. According to the legend, "Once you go in, you never come out." There are many stories of ghosts that roam the halls and basement of the Goings, either from suicides or murders. Sam and Maggie Goings are shown here around 1937 at their home at 404 Warren Avenue.

Downtown Gillette Avenue has always been the location of citywide parades. Other parade photographs similar to this one are dated 1949. Notice spectators on the rooftops of the Goings Hotel and McCracken's Store.

The Sands Motor Lodge, at Second Street and Highway 59, exemplified the new look in hotels in the early 1960s. The Sands featured a package liquor store, a swimming pool, and a restaurant. The bar was decorated with black leather booths and tapestries on the walls. The restaurant and lounge opened in 1961, with the hotel opening in 1963.

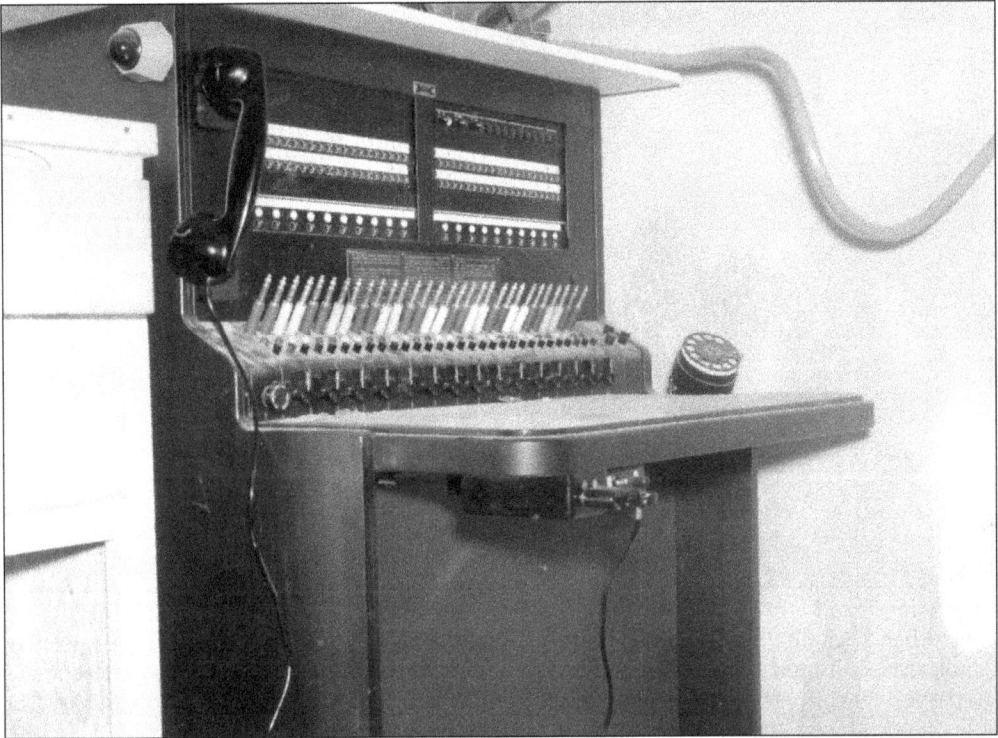

This "modern" switchboard served the Sands Motor Lodge when it opened in 1963.

The white building on the left is the Rodman Hotel. Douglas "Ike" Hayden had his barbershop in the front of the hotel. He and his wife, Alta Vivian, agreed to sell the hotel so Stockmen's Bank could build there, on the condition that Ike could have a barbershop in the new building as long as he wanted. It was just a verbal agreement, but it has stood the test of time. There is a barbershop continuing that tradition today.

The Arrowhead Motel, which was still in operation in 2009, was purchased in 1958 by Ralph Kintz when his failing health forced him to sell his ranch and move to Gillette. He completely rebuilt the facility and changed the name from Midway Court to the Arrowhead as a reflection of his passion for collecting arrowheads. He even built a large office to hold his firearm and artifact collections. The oil boom hit, and business was good!

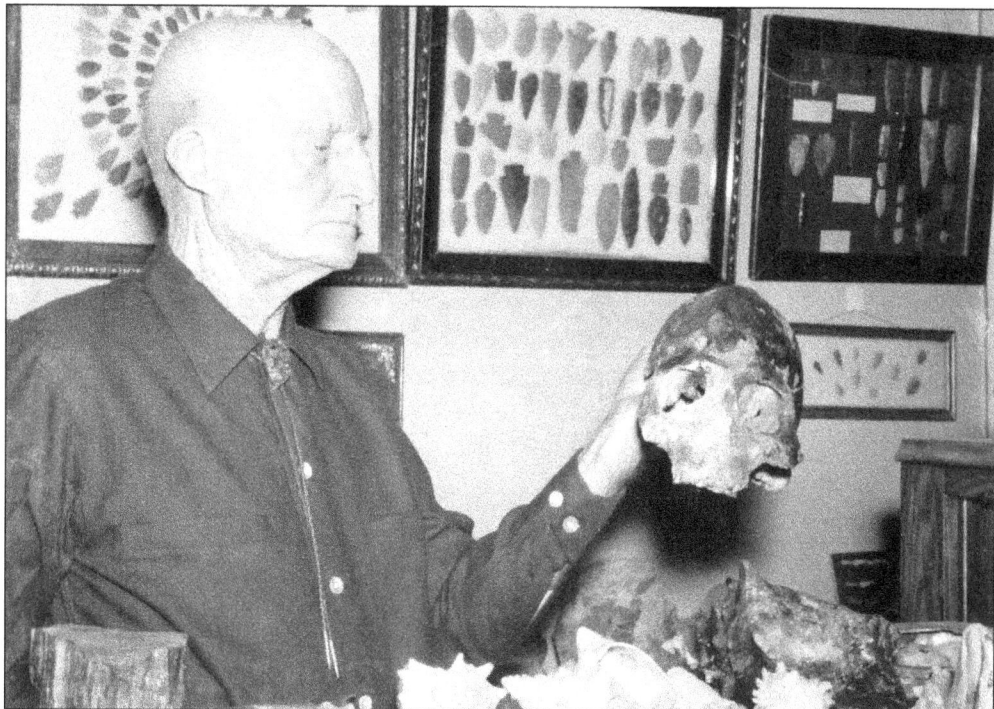

Another avid collector of Native American artifacts was L. H. Barlow, shown here holding a human skull in 1964. Barlow collected hundreds of arrowheads and other keepsakes, creating a museum in his home that he was happy to show to guests at any time.

Wilhelm's Service Station, at Second Street and Kendrick Avenue, served the tourist industry with its Pioneer Indian Museum in the early 1940s. Dale C. Wilhelm was a collector of Native American artifacts, bells, and uniform buttons, some of which were donated to the Wyoming State Museum. Wilhelm homesteaded in the Thunder Basin area of Campbell County in 1917.

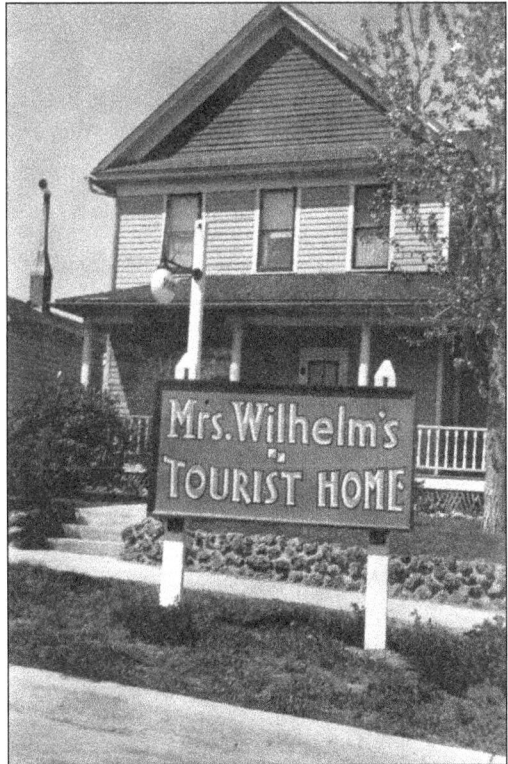

Mrs. Dale Wilhelm, the former Alice Eppes, offered another lodging option through the 1940s for visitors at her tourist home at 504 Gillette Avenue. Gillette had several homes that became boardinghouses, sometimes after the man of the house had passed away.

Before the Campbell County Rockpile Museum was opened, the Weltner Wonder Museum was one of several museums in Gillette available to tourists. Robert T. Carson and his wife, Frances, moved the Weltner Wonder Museum from Hardin, Montana, to Gillette in the 1960s. It was located on Highway 59, across from the current K-Mart. (Courtesy of Randy Thomas.)

Ralph Kintz is pictured here on the right with his wife, Dot, and son James in 1970. Ralph was instrumental in the creation of the Campbell County Rockpile Museum. He bought the land that the Rockpile was on and gave it to the county for a museum site. The original board consisted of Ralph Kintz, president; John Hines, treasurer; and Jim Bishop, secretary. The museum opened on July 21, 1974, featuring the Kintz Room, which housed his firearm and arrowhead collections.

Located at 900 West Second Street, the Campbell County Rockpile Museum was established to collect, preserve, and interpret the history of the county and region. As a result of the support, vision, and dedication of present and past county commissioners, museum board members, and staff, the museum has tripled in size and has built up a 19,000-item collection since its beginning.

Whether shooting for bounty money or sport, hunting has long been a popular pastime in the area surrounding Gillette. Some hunters had trouble telling a pronghorn antelope from a deer—or a cow. In 1960, a Pennsylvania hunter shot a cow on the Richard Dunlap place, south of Gillette, when it was in the line of fire behind some moving pronghorns. (Courtesy of Randy Thomas.)

Coyote pelts brought both bounty money and pelt money. In the 1930s and 1940s, many families made their grocery money by shooting coyotes that killed sheep. Bounty money was put up by the Wyoming Woolgrower's Association.

Jackrabbits were considered a pest on ranches, and drives were organized to kill them. A jackrabbit drive was a social event, published in the newspaper, and it involved a picnic lunch. One hundred or more rabbits would be eliminated on a single drive.

Dalbey Memorial Park was dedicated in June 1968 to the late Mayor Denzil J. "Peanuts" Dalbey, who had a soft spot for anything that benefitted children. The city experienced tremendous growth during Dalbey's six terms as mayor, which required infrastructure developments, such as streets and sewer, power, and water lines; however, Dalbey also made a point of creating a fishing lake and park to be enjoyed by Gillette's families.

Before 1962, Gillette's tourist traffic traveled on Highways 14 and 16. Local service stations, tourist home operators, and the state-run "Port of Welcome" reported many years with heavy visitor traffic. Gillette's visitors have consistently come from the east going to the west. Most visitors stayed the previous night in Rapid City, touring the Black Hills, before coming to Gillette. From here, they went on to Yellowstone Park, so Gillette has always provided a convenient central stopping place for east-west travel. Interstate 90 between Buffalo and Gillette opened in October 1962; it was built at a cost of $300,000 per mile. More than 1,500 people attended the ribbon-cutting ceremony, including from left to right Harold Del Monte, chairman of the Wyoming Highway Commission; Mayor O. W. Lusher of Buffalo; and Mayor Denzil J. "Peanuts" Dalbey of Gillette. E. W. Record stands on the stage. Interstate 90 east of Gillette would not be completed until October 1976.

Hundreds of people attended the annual Mixer Day BBQ, sponsored by the chamber of commerce, in downtown Gillette. The event was a way of saying thank you for the business during the past year. From this view, Ryan's Furniture, the V-R Trading Post, Coast to Coast, and Gambles are visible in the 200 block of Gillette Avenue in August 1959.

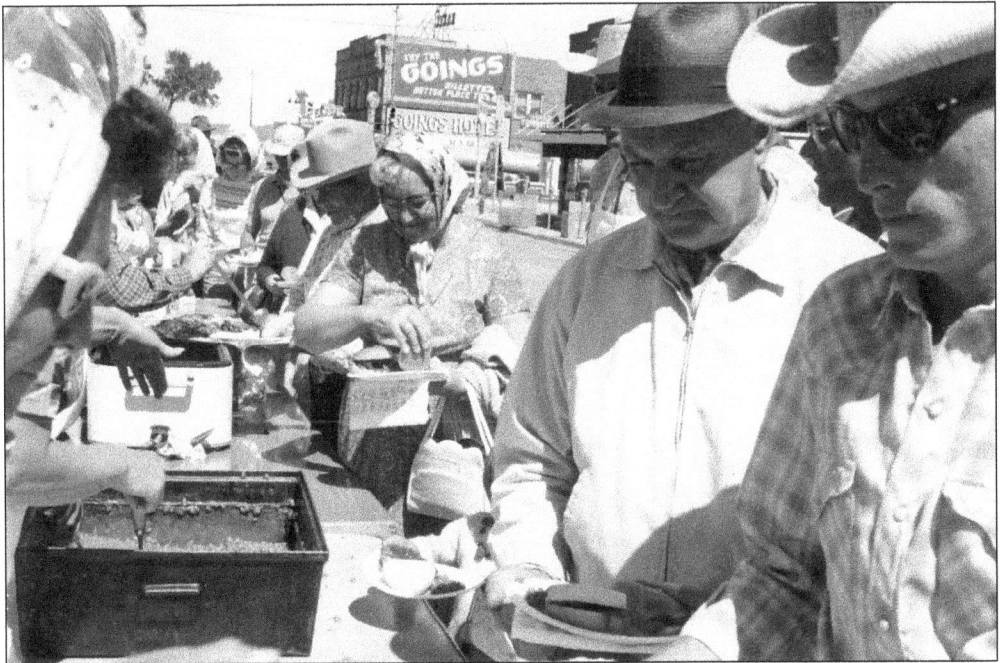

More than 2,800 people crowded downtown for a free meal at the Lamb-B-Q on August 22, 1964. The event was sponsored by the Campbell County Wool Growers Association and Auxiliary.

Sometimes folks just had to make their own fun. This photograph had "Two old soaks" written on the back of it and indicated it was taken at a hunting party in 1943.

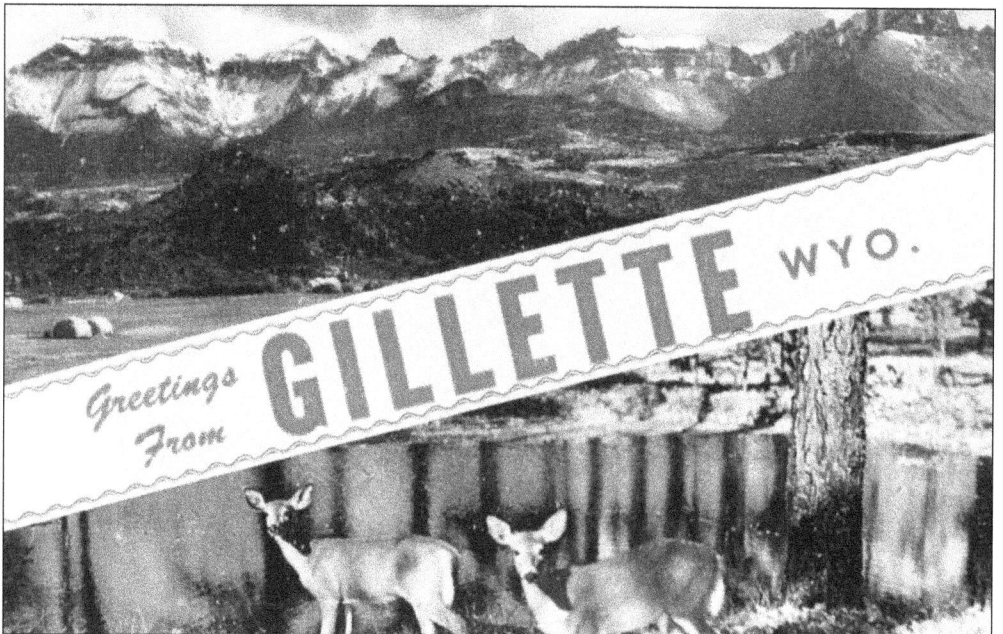

Someone with either a sense of humor or wishful thinking designed this postcard showing mountains as part of the Gillette scenery. As much as Gillette residents would love mountains surrounding the town, the nearest mountains are at least 50 miles away. (Courtesy of Randy Thomas.)

Eight

ENERGY CAPITAL OF THE NATION

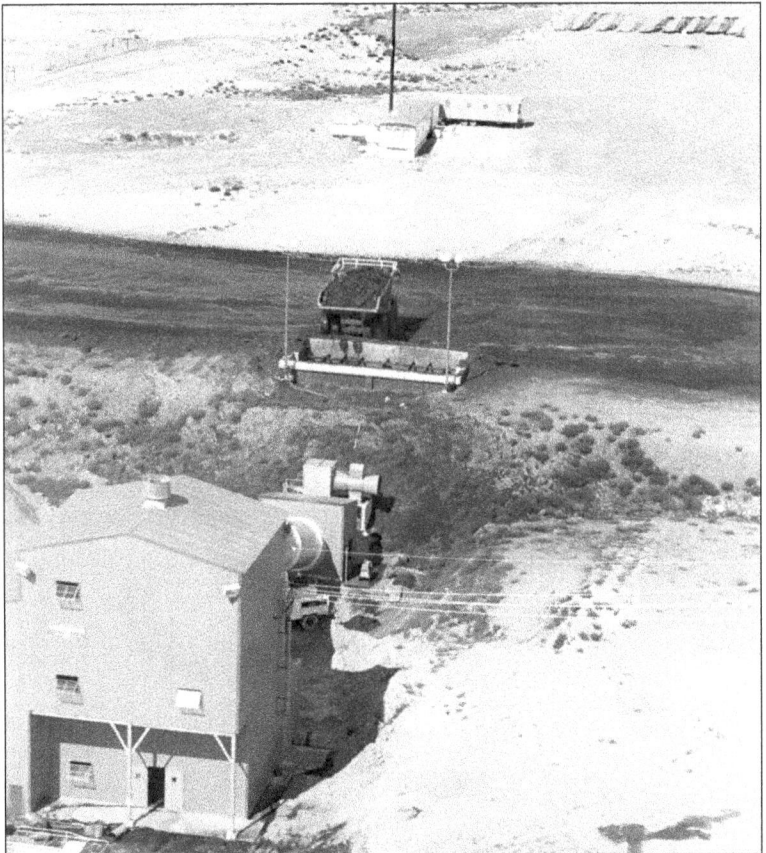

The Belle Ayr Mine, owned by AMAX Coal Company, was the second surface mine to operate in the Powder River Basin. The first was the Wyodak Mine. Test shipments of coal rolled out of Belle Ayr the last week of October 1972, bound for the Iowa Power and Light Company. The mine area was completed before the offices. Temporary offices were in the trailers at the top of the photograph. (Courtesy of Alpha Natural Resources.)

The Belle Ayr Mine is located 18 miles south of Gillette. In 1975, the number of employees was expected to be approximately 150, with a peak of 550 employees in 1979. In 1973, when the energy crisis was just beginning to threaten, the Wyoming Department of Economic Planning and Development projected Campbell County's population as increasing to nearly 15,000 by 1975; then 29,000 by 1980; 43,000 by 1985; and finally 57,000 by 1990. The actual population in 1980 was 12,134, and in 1990, it was 17,635. The reason for Gillette's growth was simple: the energy industry was looking to coal. (Courtesy of Alpha Natural Resources.)

The Belle Ayr Mine acquired a bucket wheel excavator in the early stages of the mine. It was primarily used for sandy overburden (dirt), but in 1976, it became the first wheel excavator to be used to load coal. It had one trained operator and was primarily run on the day shift. (Courtesy of Alpha Natural Resources.)

Shovel No. 6 at the Belle Ayr Mine is a 295 Bucyrus Erie shovel. In this picture it is loading a Unit Rig 120-ton truck. In 1993, the cab was raised 6 feet to allow it to better load the new 240-ton trucks. This unit is still primarily a coal-loading shovel at Belle Ayr and has undergone many modifications to keep pace with new technology and larger equipment. (Courtesy of Alpha Natural Resources.)

The Belle Ayr Mine has four silos, each with a capacity of 10,400 tons. In 1976, a train is being loaded with a capacity of 9,600 tons. This train is being flood loaded while moving through the silo at 0.75 miles per hour. This train is destined for Wisconsin Power and Light's Columbia Energy Station in Portage, Wisconsin. Current trains have a capacity in excess of 15,000 tons. (Courtesy of Alpha Natural Resources.)

This homestead of Achiel De Maegt, a Belgian immigrant, was built around 1915 and is located adjacent to the Belle Ayr Mine. The homestead house has 20-inch walls constructed out of scoria rock and mortared with natural mud from the area. This site still conveys the sense of homesteading on the grasslands of the Powder River Basin in 1915. The house, sheep corrals, and another wall are still on the property. (Courtesy of Alpha Natural Resources.)

Coal from the new Cordero Mine in the Powder River Basin moved up enclosed conveyor belts, through two crushers, and into giant silos, where it was deposited into 100-car coal trains moving under the silos at 0.5 miles per hour, for shipment to San Antonio, Texas. The above photograph shows Silo Nos. 3 and 4 in the early stages of construction on July 29, 1975. The image at right reveals the size of the nearly completed silos compared to the cement trucks on the ground. (Both, courtesy of Cloud Peak Energy.)

Reclamation legislation was written to protect the nation's environment and still allow for the recovery of the coal. This photograph of the Cordero Mine shows construction of a stream diversion channel to alter the course of the stream away from the land to be mined. (Courtesy of Cloud Peak Energy.)

Wildlife abounds on mine property. Whether they know it or not, they are safe there, as public hunting is not allowed. Most mines are home to pronghorn antelope and mule deer like the one shown here, and a few mines can claim a small elk herd. (Courtesy of Cloud Peak Energy.)

Hydroseeding is one option for curbing erosion and creating a more attractive landscape on the prairie. Hydroseeding at the Cordero Mine took place in May 1976, while part of the office building was still in the steel girder stage. (Courtesy of Cloud Peak Energy.)

Plant superintendent Keith Shelstad christens the first train loaded at the Cordero Mine on December 15, 1976. At this time, the mine was operated by Sunoco Energy Development Company (SUNEDCO), an operating unit of the Sun Company (formerly the Sun Oil Company). (Courtesy of Cloud Peak Energy.)

A special dedication was held in November 1976 for nine school projects that were recently completed to accommodate the influx of students during the boom of the 1970s. Before new schools were built, children were educated in church basements, community halls, and any available space that could be used as a classroom. This photograph is of Little Powder Elementary, one of the new schools.

Gerald Rainwater, Jim Daly, and Herb Carter celebrate receipt of a donation from the Exxon Corporation to help fund the future of Gillette College. From left to right, Rainwater and Carter served on the college advisory board; Daly was on the foundation board. (Courtesy of Gillette College.)

For many years, Gillette College held classes in the former hospital buildings on Seventh Street. Those buildings were torn down in 2008, and the new Cottonwood Apartments were constructed on that site. (Courtesy of Gillette College.)

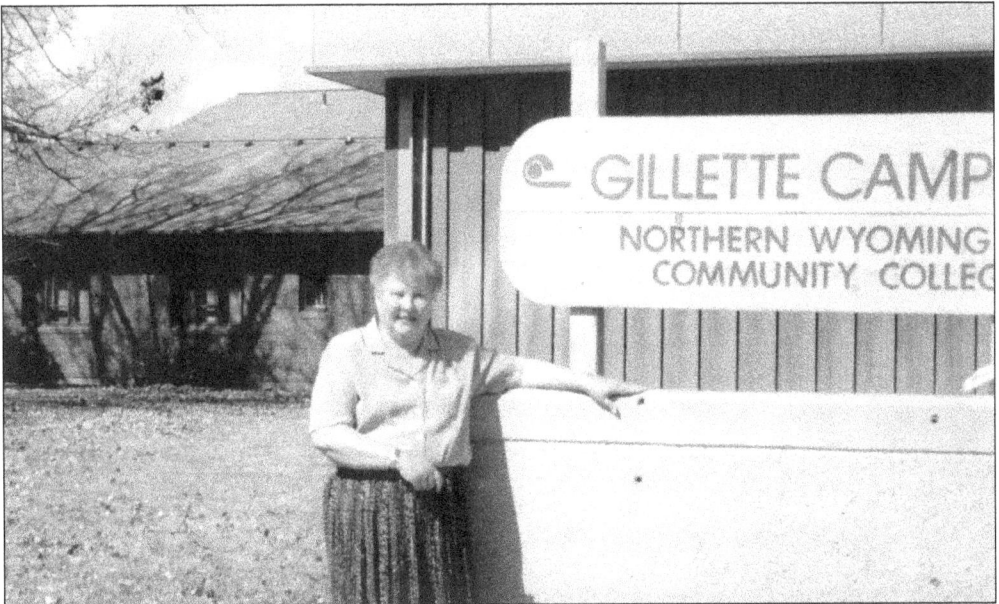

Dorothy Carter poses by the Gillette College sign in 1973. Dorothy and Herb Carter were huge supporters of higher education in Gillette. The nursing building at the college, on Enzi Drive, is named the Herbert A. and Dorothy P. Carter Health Science Education Center, in memory of the Carters. (Courtesy of Gillette College.)

Dr. D. G. Dunbar began working at the Gillette Veterinary Clinic in August 1960. He purchased the practice and the buildings in 1965. In this picture, he is working buffalo at a ranch south of Gillette. Dr. Dunbar served the community of Gillette and Campbell County for 37 years. (Courtesy of the Dunbar family.)

Nine

EVERYONE HAS A STORY

The first church built in Gillette was the First Baptist Church, pictured here at 306 Kendrick Avenue in 1903. The pastor in 1912 was Rev. C. W. Harris, who was involved in a civic movement to run some unsavory characters out of Gillette, who had given Gillette the reputation of the toughest place in Wyoming. Efforts to intimidate the parson led to him carrying a gun, and he earned the questionable privilege of being the first person arrested in the newly formed Campbell County for carrying a handgun.

Joseph Ernest "Joe" Lynde was born on March 8, 1911, on a homestead 20 miles south of Gillette. He learned the sheep-ranching business from his father, Isaac Worth Lynde, and went into ranching for himself in 1934. Drought and the Depression forced him to other pursuits, including running heavy equipment, operating a bentonite business, and owning the Blue Diamond Coal Mine. The heavy equipment was moved to a home base in Dubois, Wyoming, in 1955. For some time, Lynde worked at cutting and clearing diseased timber in the mountains for the U.S. Forest Service, where his fellow workers christened him "Timber Jack." Lynde became enamored with the mountain man culture, so he parked his heavy equipment and began running traplines and living the life of a mountain man. That is when he received the label of being the eccentric Timber Jack Joe Lynde. Timber Jack and his English sheep dog, Tuffy, appeared in three movies, in numerous stage, television, and radio appearances, and in parades. Their work has benefitted children, the handicapped, and senior citizens. (Courtesy of Wright Centennial Museum.)

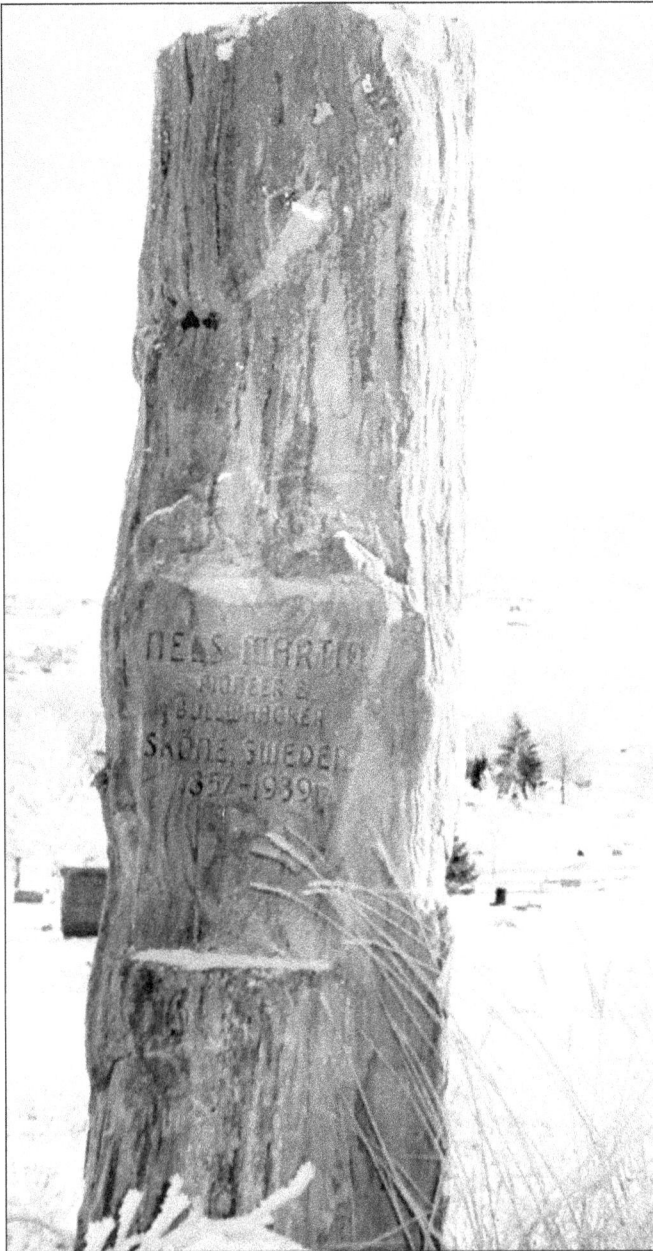

This unusual grave marker is for Nels Martin, a Swedish immigrant who moved to the United States in 1869. He found work in the Dakota Territory as a bull-whacker, hauling freight for the gold rush in the Black Hills. Bull-whackers did not ride on the wagons but walked along side. Martin said that he never needed patches on the seat of his pants, but he sure did wear out shoe leather. When he heard the railroad was coming to Gillette, he moved here to start a freighting business. One of the first jobs he had was freighting lumber into Gillette for the Daly brothers to build a store. Before the building was completed Martin was on the trail to bring in a wagon train load of supplies to stock the Daly brothers' store. He freighted in and around this area for the next 10 years. Martin filed on a homestead west of Gillette but lost the land and his cabin in a sheriff's sale to pay his gambling debts. He passed away in July 1937.

Bunk Haynes (pictured at far right) was a black man raised by a white family in Texas. He moved to Wyoming after the Civil War, "where even women were treated as equals," according to the book *The Treasured Years*. He came up the trail with the Matthews family, who settled and built the T-7 Ranch on the Belle Fourche River in northeastern Wyoming. Haynes homesteaded 480 acres on Donkey Creek south and east of Gillette. This area now includes the land from the Holiday Plaza to the Fishing Lake and east, including the Country Club. He was a good cook and a neat housekeeper. He died of liver cancer on August 17, 1917.

In 1892, Diamond L. Slim ran a 12-horse jerkline freighting business in Gillette. His real name was W. C. Clifton, but he was called Diamond L. Slim because he worked a while at the Diamond L Ranch near Newcastle and he was tall and slender. Diamond L. was infamous for the 1903 murder of a young married couple, John and Louella Church. He became indebted to the couple, and when settlement was due, he repaid them with death handed out in the saddle room of a granary. He buried the bodies and bedded down a band of sheep over their graves to hide any evidence.

Diamond L. Slim was arrested after he tried to sell some of the jewelry belonging to Louella Church. Deputy sheriff Lew Jenne secured a confession from Slim and the location of the bodies. The group shown above is thought to be the ones who discovered the graves. Slim was kept in the jail at Newcastle until he could have a trial. A posse of 35 cowboys stormed the jail, grabbed Slim, and took him to a bridge nearby. Diamond L. Slim's only words were, "Boys, I'm not a murderer." The posse then put the rope around his neck and tossed him over the bridge. The jerk completely decapitated him.

George Amos was the foreman of the Keeline's 4-J Ranch in the early 1880s. He never wore a gun or boots, and he never married. He swore, drank, and gambled. In his will, he left "$1,000 to Guy "Bum-a-Nickle" Garrett, who had loaned him money but never asked him to pay it back.

George Amos enjoyed reading anything he could find, and he seemed to remember everything he read. When he died in 1929, he gave his entire estate to build a library. The amount of the estate was $21,197, just $2,000 short of the amount needed to construct the library building, now located on Gillette Avenue and known as the George Amos Memorial Building. It served as the only library for Gillette until 1983, when the new library was built on 4-J Road. Without a large enough population to support two libraries, this library closed down around 1993.

"Gillette is the best town of its size or any other size in the state," according to Roy Montgomery in 1947. He should know; he was unique in his involvement in Gillette. Montgomery was admitted to the bar in Kansas but never entered the legal profession. One record of his life indicated, "His knowledge of law has been of immense value to him in the conduct of his business affairs."

Thomas LeRoy "Roy" Montgomery was arrested in 1915 in Wyoming for white slavery. He served a two-year term at Leavenworth, Kansas, where he had this photograph taken, showing his best side. He served as mayor of Gillette from 1914 to 1915 and again from 1936 to 1944. (Courtesy of National Archives.)

The Pea Green was Gillette's brothel, which was owned by Roy Montgomery. His involvement with the Pea Green led to his arrest for white slavery in 1915. Montgomery also owned the *Gillette News* from 1912 to 1916. In his newspaper, Montgomery declared he was being persecuted not for his ownership of a brothel, but for being a Democrat.

Roy Montgomery moved to the Gillette area around 1903. In 1905, he owned a semiprofessional baseball team that practiced "way out of town," now Seventh Street and Gillette Avenue. Montgomery hired men who could play baseball to work for him in one of his many businesses when they were not playing baseball.

Roy Montgomery was one of the foremost cattle and horse ranchers in Campbell County and was also the proprietor of the Montgomery Hotel for five years. In 1917, upon his return from Leavenworth, Kansas, he opened the Gillette Hotel (formerly the Pea Green). Montgomery also had extensive investments in oil lands, which provided him income later in his life.

Known affectionately as "Mexican John," John Marroquin came to Wyoming in 1877. He worked "doggies" on several ranches, staying with the Keelines for most of the time. When the Keelines sold the ranch, Mexican John continued to make the ranch his home until his death in 1946. He was considered one of the best ropers in the area.

The Homestead Doctor is the name of the book written by Dr. Archie Gray Hoadley about his life and medical practice in Campbell County. It is estimated that during his years of practice he delivered between 3,000 and 4,000 babies. Dr. Hoadley established a hospital in Gillette and also the Medical Art Clinic with his son Dr. Joe Hoadley. Dr. A. G. Hoadley is shown here on the lower step of an early hospital on Ross Avenue, with Dr. E. E. Baker on the higher step.

Shields Wright, otherwise known as White Eagle, came to Gillette from Oklahoma in the summer of 1909. Although he could not hear or speak, he was educated well enough to write a cookbook entitled The Gillette Cook Book in 1916. Recipes were contributed by the ladies of the community, but the book also contained notes about the town and citizens, and there were original poems written by White Eagle.

George Raymond Eisele, seaman second class, U.S. Naval Reserve, received the Purple Heart posthumously for staying at his gun in the face of an onrushing Japanese torpedo airplane in the Soloman Islands on November 11, 1942. (Courtesy of William J. Eisele.)

The USS *Eisele*, a destroyer escort ship, was named after George Raymond Eisele. The Campbell County Rockpile Museum displays a collection of his medals, letters, photographs, flags, and the christening bottle used to dedicate the destroyer escort. (Courtesy of William J. Eisele.)

The matriarch of the Underwood family, Beulah Underwood, wanted to reward people for their good deeds. When a Gillette resident was in the newspaper for something good they had done, Beulah Underwood would mail them the newspaper clipping with a piece of chewing gum. The gum was her "signature" for something worth rewarding. Dressed all in black, Underwood would often walk Gillette Avenue passing out gum to people she would meet on the street. She is pictured here on Easter Sunday, April 11, 1971. (Courtesy of the Underwood family.)

Henry "Tiny" Fritzler came to Gillette in 1953 because he wanted to be a policeman and work with kids. He first worked as an ice-cream man four days a week. Sometimes kids would ask him if he needed any help, and he would let them help him load the truck. After they were finished, Fritzler would treat them to popsicles. He started on the police force in 1956, working as a night officer seven days a week, 12 hours a night. Fritzler went to schools and handed out treats to the younger children and gave bicycle safety books to the older children. He played the traditional Santa at Christmastime. He received many awards for his outstanding contributions to the children of Campbell County. Pictured from left to right are Henry "Tiny" Fritzler, Robert Harper, James Kincaid, Chief Louis Pappas, Orville Sherrard, Lloyd Shane, and John Quarterman.

It seems the West attracted some real characters. Monikers tell a story, along with the fact there were so many of them. Unique names found during research for this book were Holdout Johnson, Every Day Johnson, Lame Smithy, Long Shorty, Shakey Ed Kelley, Booster Jim, Red O'Neil, Woodbox Jim, Kid Highly, Rattlesnake Jack, Coyote Bill, Scrub Peeler, and Bum-a-Nickel Garrett. This photograph of a relatively normal looking cowboy shows Pecos Johnny Allison, who would be one of the founders of Stockmen's Bank and would serve two terms in the house of representatives.

33904

J. W. BENSON
WYOMING COWBOY ARTIST

Jacob William "Jake" Benson was born on May 10, 1895, in Thurman, Iowa. His family moved to Wyoming, near Hulett, in 1903. He was an all-around cowboy, learning how to ride, build fence, and put up hay. He was also a carpenter and a self-taught artist. Benson painted many Western murals, including one that adorned the walls of the Elite Bar in Gillette for many years. Another of his murals still hangs in the Campbell County Rockpile Museum as of 2009. He died in Newcastle on December 11, 1958, at the age of 63.

BIBLIOGRAPHY

Bowden, Margaret. *1916 Wyoming, Here We Come!* Cheyenne, WY: Pioneer Printing, 2002.

Bragg, William Jr. *Pre-Centennial Campbell County.* April 8, 1976.

———. *Campbell County: The Slumbering Giant.* Gillette, WY: Holiday Inn, 1978.

Bartlett, I. S. *History of Wyoming.* Chicago: S. J. Clarke Publishing Company, 1918.

Campbell County Cemetery District. *Whispers From the Past.* March 1997.

Campbell County High School yearbooks, various years.

Campbell County High School English Class 1983–1984. *Campbell County Chronicles: The Way We Were.* 1984.

Campbell County Historical Society. *The Treasured Years.* Marceline, MO: Walsworth Publishing Company, 1991.

Gardiner, Steve. *Rumblings From Razor City: The Oral History of Gillette, Wyoming, An Energy Boom Town.* Self-published, 1985.

King, Robert A. *Trails to Rails: A History of Wyoming's Railroads.* Casper, WY: Endeavor Books, 2003.

Nelson, Dick J. *A 'B and M' Excursion 1893 and 'Northern Wyoming.'* Nairobi, Kenya: William Kilpatrick Purdy publisher, 1966.

Ricketts, Louis D. *Annual Report of the Territorial Geologist to the Governor of Wyoming.* Cheyenne, WY: The Cheyenne Daily Leader Steam Book Print, 1890.

Sheridan County Extension Homemakers Council. *Sheridan County Heritage Book.* Pierre, SD: The State Publishing Company, 1983.

The Wyoming Newspaper Project.

INDEX

Visit us at
arcadiapublishing.com

www.ingramcontent.com/pod-product-compliance
Lightning Source LLC
Chambersburg PA
CBHW050626110426
42813CB00007B/1725